Early Vehic

C000098658

Peter W

A Shire book

Published in 2004 by Shire Publications Ltd,
Cromwell House, Church Street, Princes Risborough,
Buckinghamshire HP27 9AA, UK.
(Website: www.shirebooks.co.uk)

British Library Cataloguing in Publication Data:
Card, Peter W.
Early vehicle lighting. – 2nd ed. – (Shire album; 185)
1. Motor vehicles – Lighting – History
2. Bicycles – Lighting – History
I. Title 629.2'71'09
ISBN 0 7478 0585 7

To Rebecca, Ruth and Rachel

Editorial Consultant: Michael E. Ware, former Director of the National
Motor Museum, Beaulieu.

ACKNOWLEDGEMENTS
The author thanks Dr Chris Brooks for his unfailing support and for the generous loan of
much original illustrative material, and David Card for his many useful comments and
acquisition support. Further help was kindly supplied by Nick Baldwin, Nicholas
Clayton, Nick Georgano, Tony Gosnell, Peter Tilley, Nick Waller, and
Adrian Brown for photography.

Cover: *The front cover of a 'Brolt' electric lighting brochure dating from 1912. The artist, Charles Sykes, has chosen to depict a Rolls-Royce 40/50 horsepower open-drive limousine and has even incorporated his own newly introduced Rolls-Royce radiator mascot, which he designed and registered in 1911.*

Title page: *A Glasgow-manufactured Howe front-steered tricycle fitted with an oil-powered tricycle lamp. Because tricycles were much slower than bicycles there was not the need for a robust parallel-sprung mounting bracket at the rear. Instead, a plain spade fitting was employed.*

Printed in Great Britain by CIT Printing Services, Press Buildings,
Merlins Bridge, Haverfordwest, Pembrokeshire SA61 1XF.

Contents

A Powell & Hanmer shop advertising board dating from c.1904. The creative ability of commercial artists at the time was boundless and certainly no less than it is today. The company hoped their advertisement would grip the imagination of the public and encourage them to purchase their product and no other. Here a goddess is seen standing on a rocky outcrop and holding aloft, for all to see, the newly designed 'Zephyr' oil-powered bicycle lamp. The depiction of the young and beautiful woman in her full-length silken gown is reminiscent of those portrayed by the then fashionable Czech artist Alphonse Mucha, whose work, with its graceful flowing lines, epitomised one aspect of the Art Nouveau style.

Introduction

The invention of vehicle lighting, whether it be for bicycle or motor car, is so closely linked to the invention of transportation during the Victorian era that a review of its history will assist in the understanding of early vehicle lighting.

The bicycle and tricycle were developed over a seventy-five-year period from 1817 to 1892, the latter date heralding the adoption of the pneumatic-tyred machine that would be easily recognisable as the predecessor of the modern bicycle.

In 1817 Baron von Drais invented the two-wheeled 'Hobbyhorse', which, although it had a short commercial life, was very popular with wealthy young bucks for around three years. Propulsion was achieved simply by pushing with the feet. While this was exhilarating for a short distance, long journeys were too exhausting to be undertaken and, in consequence, there was no need for lighting at night.

Ernest and Pierre Michaux of Paris were responsible for the vital development that gave the bicycle its own means of propulsion. They had rediscovered the two-wheeled idea and fitted cranks to the front wheel of a bicycle in 1863. Generically named the 'Vélocipède', the design was later perfected by Eugene Meyer, and slowly but surely these bicycles became more comfortable to ride and began to be used as everyday transport. Rides into the suburbs and hamlets after dark became commonplace and from about 1868 the manufacturers of Vélocipèdes offered a front lamp as an optional extra.

The 'Ordinary' or 'high-wheel' bicycle slowly developed from the Vélocipède and from about this time clubs were formed to promote comradeship and present a collective voice among enthusiasts. One of the first clubs to be inaugurated was the Pickwick Bicycle Club in 1870. Still in existence in 2004, the club continues to promote the same camaraderie and friendship that existed when it was founded.

Cycle lighting

Oil lamps

Nineteenth-century photographs of machines and riders show a varied and strange array of lamps, usually fitted to the steering head. If they were not carefully mounted, these lamps, which were often adaptations of oil-powered domestic lanterns, frequently came loose and jammed in the front wheel, bringing the rider down over the handlebars and landing him on his head.

The roads during this time were full of potholes, strewn with stones and covered in a thick layer of dust or mud. Signposts were rare and there was little street lighting, even in towns. The first British cycling magazine, *Bicycling News*, appeared in January 1876. Every week it carried detailed reports of pleasure rides organised by the cycling clubs and as summer approached evening rides began to appear in club itineraries, increasing the demand for better-designed forms of lighting equipment.

It was soon discovered that a lamp placed in a lower position, attached to the axle hub of the large front wheel of an Ordinary (high-wheel) bicycle, gave a beam that was not only closer to the road but

A 'Zephyr' Ordinary of around 1877 made by Tom Harris of London with an 'Albion' – a hub lamp of the 'simple style' – fitted on the hub of the large wheel. The subtlety of design allows the lamp to be pointed down slightly in order to aid the beam of light to shine on the road just ahead of the rider. Being an early machine, this bicycle has only forty spokes in its front wheel. Several years later the number of spokes in the driving wheel would increase to sixty or, sometimes, eighty and consequently a large square-pattern lamp of this type would be impossible to push between the narrow spokes; this is when the 'divided style' of hub lamp became popular.

The 'long hot summer' of the Edwardian period before the hostilities of the First World War was a time of serene and carefree days, characterised by congestion-free open roads, made exciting by the use of personal transport and even more memorable by being able to travel long distances at night. This Joseph Lucas Limited advertising poster dating from 1905 depicts a 'King of the Road' bicycle oil lamp illuminating a distance well beyond its actual penetrating power. The John Masefield poem 'Roadways' captures the mood of the period:

'My road calls me, lures me
West, east, south and north;
Most roads lead men homewards,
My road leads me forth.'

also much more effective. The first hub lamps were made of tinplate in a square design, with a hinged barrel at the top that swung open to fit over the axle hub. A stout wire with leather washers fitted at either end served as an adjustment for lateral movement inside the wheel. These lamps are now identified as the 'simple style' and first appeared in 1876. The power source was either paraffin oil or colza oil and a clean open-weave wick was needed to allow for a good capillary action.

Edward Salsbury of the Salsbury Lamp Works, Long Acre, London, claimed the hub lamp as his invention. By 1878 Joseph Lucas of Birmingham was also making hub lamps and by 1880 had developed an improved design, the 'divided style', which continued to be offered in catalogues until at least 1894. Although these divided-style hub lamps were much larger and could hold more oil they nevertheless solved the problem of trying to insert a box shape through the narrow spokes of the Ordinary bicycle's front wheel – indeed, by 1880 the number of spokes used in the front wheel of bicycles had increased, making the gap between each spoke even narrower. Lucas's lamps were manufactured in two halves and hinged at the top, and so, when opened up, they provided a narrower profile for insertion between the spokes. After entry into the wheel the lamp was simply dropped over the hub, the front and rear halves clipping together at the base. By

An illustration of a divided-style hub lamp fitted inside the large front wheel of an Ordinary bicycle. In this position the lamp offered a safe place from which to illuminate the road; indeed the rider would see the shadow of the wheel rim on the road ahead of him. On the other hand, an oncoming pedestrian would see a flashing light coming towards him as a result of the lamp's oscillation as the wheel spun around. The hub lamp fitted is an example of Joseph Lucas & Sons' 'King of the Road' model, an inspired name applied to the Birmingham company's best-quality lamps. Priced at about £1 each, or 30 shillings (£1.50) for a brass and nickel-plated example, its purchase would have been a significant expenditure. However, because of their superior construction these lamps offered many years of use; indeed around 90 per cent of the numerous hub lamps that survive today are of Joseph Lucas manufacture.

1882 mechanical or winding wick holders were in common use, which not only aided wick adjustment but also allowed for a greater degree of flame control and, in consequence, a more efficient use of oil.

The idea of a more user-friendly bicycle with a riding position nearer the ground and the rear wheel driven by chain had been written about as early as 1869 but the 'safety bicycle' was not commercially available until 1885, after a number of false starts. The first of the breed, the 'Rover' bicycle, set the design style for machines with two wheels of a similar size, such as we would recognise today. As the safety bicycle was developed, so specifically designed lamps were introduced. The lamps were large and cumbersome like the hub lamps but had a parallel-sprung bracket fitted at the rear. These 'safety lamps' were still capacious because of the need for a high volume of air to circulate around the wick so as to keep the lamp alight in difficult and often windy conditions. Although the parallel-sprung bracket helped to even out the jarring and bumping caused by the narrow solid-rubber tyres it was important to use a good-quality, free-flowing oil and a clean, dry wick to ensure a good, bright light.

This Thomas Smith & Sons oil headlamp dating from around 1880 has several interesting features. In an attempt to produce an effective anti-vibration device, two spring-loaded pistons are placed at the rear and joined to a wire tongue for attaching to the steering head of an Ordinary bicycle. The Teutonic finial serves no purpose except to give the lamp a certain aristocratic dignity.

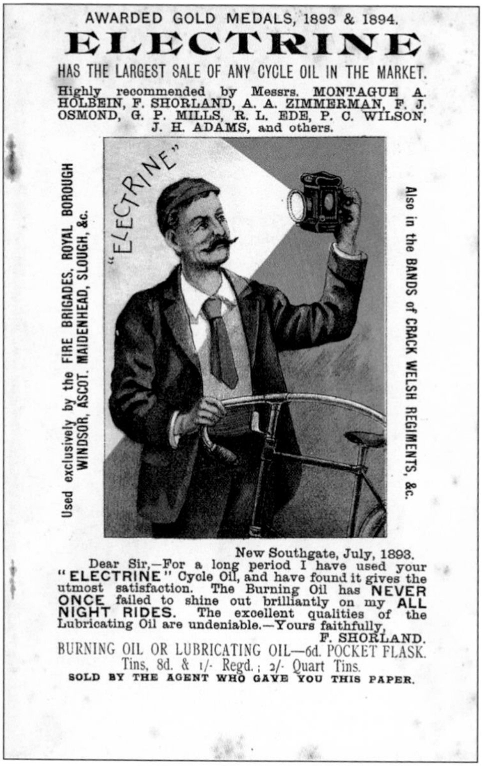
AWARDED GOLD MEDALS, 1893 & 1894.
ELECTRINE
HAS THE LARGEST SALE OF ANY CYCLE OIL IN THE MARKET.
Highly recommended by Messrs. MONTAGUE A. HOLBEIN, F. SHORLAND, A. A. ZIMMERMAN, F. J. OSMOND, G. P. MILLS, R. L. EDE, P. C. WILSON, J. H. ADAMS, and others.
"ELECTRINE"
Used exclusively by the FIRE BRIGADES, ROYAL BOROUGH WINDSOR, ASCOT, MAIDENHEAD, SLOUGH, &c.
Also in the BANDS of CRACK WELSH REGIMENTS, &c.
New Southgate, July, 1893.
Dear Sir,—For a long period I have used your "ELECTRINE" Cycle Oil, and have found it gives the utmost satisfaction. The Burning Oil has NEVER ONCE failed to shine out brilliantly on my ALL NIGHT RIDES. The excellent qualities of the Lubricating Oil are undeniable.—Yours faithfully,
F. SHORLAND.
BURNING OIL OR LUBRICATING OIL—6d. POCKET FLASK.
Tins, 8d. & 1/- Regd.; 2/- Quart Tins.
SOLD BY THE AGENT WHO GAVE YOU THIS PAPER.

An Electrine oil advertising handbill dating from around 1895. Because cycling was so popular at this time the manufacturers of lamp oil made more money from their regular sales of oil than the lamp manufacturers made from the sale of the lamp.

A variation of the safety lamp was manufactured specifically for tricycles. The same box-like construction was used but, because tricycles were slower, more stable and less prone to vibration than bicycles, the rear mounting bracket was different. A solid yoke was riveted to the rear of the lamp and this was pushed on to a vertical spade-shaped bracket. Pairs of these lamps could be purchased for mounting either side of the seated rider, but owing to the wheel configuration of

Below: *H. Miller & Company manufactured domestic lamps from 1869 and turned to bicycle-lamp manufacture in around 1883. This page from the firm's 1888 catalogue shows (from left to right) an oil-powered safety lamp unusually mounted on the front-wheel axle extension of a safety bicycle, a profile of the safety lamp with prices, and a divided-style hub lamp.*

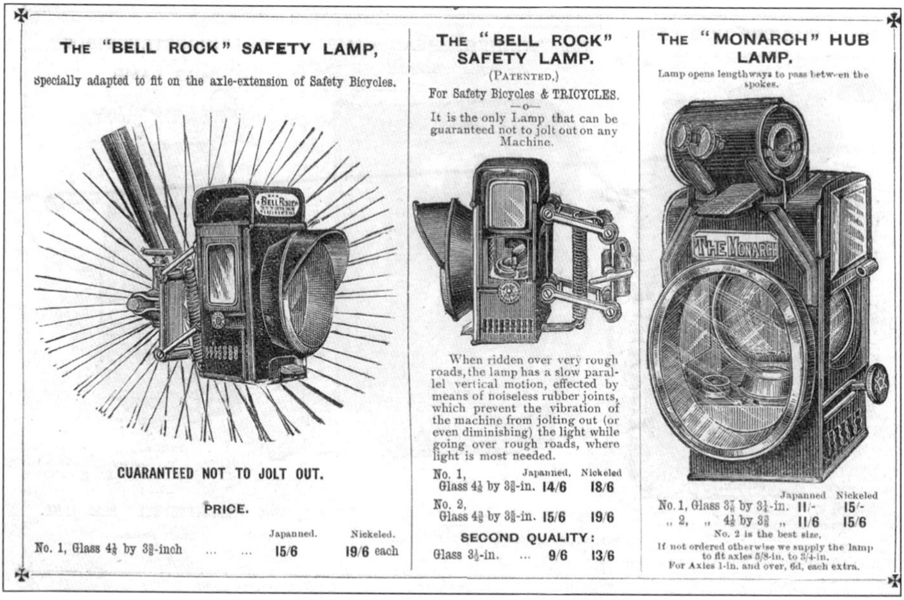
THE "BELL ROCK" SAFETY LAMP,
Specially adapted to fit on the axle-extension of Safety Bicycles.
BELL ROCK
GUARANTEED NOT TO JOLT OUT.
PRICE.
Japanned. Nickeled.
No. 1, Glass 4½ by 3⅝-inch ... ... 15/6 19/6 each
THE "BELL ROCK" SAFETY LAMP.
(PATENTED,)
For Safety Bicycles & TRICYCLES.
It is the only Lamp that can be guaranteed not to jolt out on any Machine.
When ridden over very rough roads, the lamp has a slow parallel vertical motion, effected by means of noiseless rubber joints, which prevent the vibration of the machine from jolting out (or even diminishing) the light while going over rough roads, where light is most needed.
No. 1, Japanned, Nickeled
Glass 4½ by 3⅝-in. 14/6 18/6
No. 2,
Glass 4⅝ by 3⅝-in. 15/6 19/6
SECOND QUALITY:
Glass 3½-in. ... 9/6 13/6
THE "MONARCH" HUB LAMP.
Lamp opens lengthways to pass between the spokes.
THE MONARCH
Japanned Nickeled
No. 1, Glass 3⅞ by 3¼-in. 11/- 15/-
" 2, " 4½ by 3⅝ " 11/6 15/6
No. 2 is the best size.
If not ordered otherwise we supply the lamp to fit axles 5/8-in. to 3/4-in.
For Axles 1-in. and over, 6d. each extra.

A solid-tyre safety bicycle fitted with a Joseph Lucas & Sons oil-powered safety lamp dating from around 1888.

the standard high-wheel tricycle, with a wheel either side of the rider, the lamps were mounted very close to each wheel. The wick winders were therefore fitted to the inner positions for ease of control while riding.

With improving road conditions and the increased use of pneumatic tyres from about 1892 it was no longer found necessary to manufacture such large, shock-resistant lamps that required a large volume of air in order to be kept alight. Slowly, over a period of four years, all cycle-lamp manufacturers began to make smaller models so that from 1895 a large range of *petit* oil lamps was being offered to the ever-increasing numbers of cyclists. Cycling was becoming more and more popular throughout Europe and America and, simultaneously, numerous groundbreaking lamp designs were being produced.

An E. Salsbury & Son 'Invincible' oil-powered safety-bicycle lamp dating from 1892. It possesses a two-faceted 'dioptic' front lens that was designed to give a wider field of illumination. Also notice the opaque moulded side glass, designed to give a glow of light to each side of the lamp. Many lamp manufacturers adopted this design feature and used various colours, including red, pink, blue, green, yellow, and clear glass. It was only after about 1900 that the colours tended to be standardised to red on the left and green on the right.

Perhaps the most impressive English-manufactured lamp was Lucas's 'Microphote' oil lamp. Harry Lucas, the guiding entrepreneur of Joseph Lucas & Sons (incorporated as Joseph Lucas Limited in 1897), had an eye for saleable design. On 25th August 1897 he patented a small oil-powered lamp that had a diagonally divided spherical central body with four triangular red and green glass segments. These were arranged separately, two on each side of the diagonal dividing line. The Microphote was initially shown at the Stanley Show and later at the National Cycle Show at the Crystal Palace in December 1897. Like so many good designs, it was copied. One firm to bring out a similar version was H. Miller & Company of Birmingham, who produced a spherical-bodied 'Miniature Lito' oil lamp, and whom Lucas was later to sue for patent infringement.

The Microphote's one limitation was that it was too small to provide a useful beam of light. It may have been an appealing lamp for the

Harry Lucas's penchant for a slick phrase and inspired advertising is reflected in this rare 1897 shop-card advertisement for the 'Microphote' oil lamp. The image alludes to a love-stricken lamp having been pierced by Cupid's arrow and attracting the interest of a young waif under a moonlit sky.

ladies and its decorativeness may have been appreciated during a moonlit ride in Battersea Park, London, but it was totally useless, as the writer can confirm, during a moonless scorch in the country. In consequence, Harry Lucas decided that because the shape of the Microphote was a marketable success he would simply double its size and create a new lamp. The new model, nearly 6 inches (152 mm) high, Lucas named the 'King Holophote'. He promoted it as being 'the great light giver' and first offered it in the 1899 wholesalers' catalogue for 15 shillings (75p). It continued in production until 1902.

German manufacturers of lamps were also prolific at this time and, while their goods reached Britain and the United States, their main

A simple but effective advertisement for the 'Solar' bicycle lamp. The 'Solar' was manufactured for twenty-nine years but the year of the lamp can often be identified by subtle changes in design. In this case the model, which is depicted in profile, has a flat top and a spherical calcium carbide bowl, fixing its date of manufacture – and therefore the date of the postcard advertisement – as 1898.

Right: *French advertisers were particularly fond of including accidents in their promotions, presumably in an effort to frighten people into buying their wares, as in the case of this advertisement for a dynamo-powered bicycle lamp.*

market-places were Scandinavia, eastern Europe and Russia. Firms such as Riemann, Pressler and Lohmann produced many models and their catalogues were large and impressive. Although most examples had unique designs, a number of lamps were almost exact copies of successful English- and American-built lamps – which, historically, is odd because German-designed lamps were quite serviceable and sound. Like the English and American manufacturers, the Germans delighted in giving their lamps attractive names, for example, 'Piccolo', 'Leuchte', 'Blitz' and 'Sirius'. One lamp offered by Windmuller was itself copied – namely, the 'Feuerball' (Fireball), which was a spherical, almost egg-shaped, oil-burning lamp with a parallel-sprung mounting bracket at the top.

England also had its favourite lamps. One particular example was the 'Silver King'. Patented by Harry Lucas in 1895, it first appeared

The 'Otto' acetylene gas lamp by Otto Scharlach of Germany. This is an example of one of the first decorated lamps, with heavy embossing and machining to the water reservoir, rear bracket and calcium carbide chamber.

Above: *A Gormully & Jeffrey 'Rambler No. 1' oil-powered safety lamp dating from 1890.*

A second-pattern example of the Bridgeport Gun Implement Company 'Tally Ho' oil lamp. The original patent dates from February 1898.

in the 1896 Lucas catalogue and continued in production, albeit modified from time to time, until 1941.

Over the years several alternatives to oil have been adopted for bicycle-lamp use, each using the reservoir and open-weave wick principal whereby fluid is drawn up the wick by capillary action. One of these alternatives was petroleum, known as 'kerosene' in the United States but certainly nothing to do with petrol. Once lit, it required an increase in oxygen to produce a bright white light and subsequently burned at a much higher temperature. Because of the impurities in its commercial manufacture and heat discharge it left a nasty sooty deposit on the rear reflector and chimney. Petroleum-burning lamps sometimes used a larger porcelain burner together with extra air vents

Inspired advertising for bicycle lamps was common at the end of the Victorian era – as in this advertisement for the Partridge & Edgar 'IC' bicycle lamp encouraging the reader to sing 'Oh, Say Can You See' to the opening bar of the 'Star-spangled Banner'.

A Joseph Lucas Limited 'Petrolet' lamp mounted on a later shop display stand.

to help dissipate the heat; to aid this, a removable pan was placed at the base of the burner in which to collect residue. These lamps can often be identified by the incorporation of 'petro' in their name – for example Lucas's 'Petrolet' and 'Petrophote' and Powell & Hanmer's 'Petro Zephyr'.

Other types of lamp with an unusual lighting medium are those using benzene. The reservoirs of the lamps, which are usually tiny and lightweight, were packed with cotton wool. A fluid not unlike modern lighter fuel was poured into the reservoir and the vapour of the liquid filtered up through a small tube. When ignited, the benzene vapour burned with a small, bright flame. This type of lamp was often kept in the pocket and used by cyclists as an emergency lamp.

An advertisement for the 'Star' oil lamp with a novel etched star motif in the front glass. Part of the fascination of collecting early vehicle lighting is the large number of curious, and sometimes bizarre, small-production lamps created before the First World War, intended to harness the new enthusiasm for travel. Manufacturers would often create a subsidiary company and turn their attention to lamp production in tandem with the production of other precision-engineered artefacts, such as rifles, clocks or domestic lighting.

An interesting but unsuccessful idea was that of the wax-burning bicycle lamp. Wax-burning domestic lamps had some success at the end of the Victorian period because of how safe they were to use around the home. Since wax remained in a solid state until it came into contact with the warm wick, the use of such a medium alleviated the danger of a paraffin-powered table lamp spilling its fluid and igniting the home. R. Chalmers & Sons of the Lion Works, Birmingham, adapted the idea and in 1907 offered a wax-burning bicycle lamp. However, the makers forgot that the exterior ambient temperature would keep the wax cold and hard, thus making it difficult to keep fluid to allow for capillary action. This type of lamp did continue in production until around 1910 but it was not a success.

Although some companies offered a lamp for mounting on the rear of a

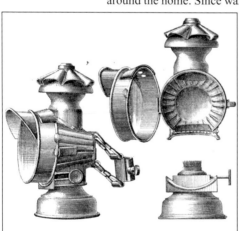

Gabriel Ducellier had been manufacturing candle and oil lamps from 1889 and won the Medaille d'Or at Paris in 1893 and two Diplômes d'Honneur in 1894 and 1895 for his designs. This image of 'La Française' depicts the 1894 winning model.

A 'Fifax' oil lamp by Worsnop's of Halifax, dating from around 1905. Although it is not visible in the photograph, this well-designed lamp possesses a circular wick that burned inside a glass tube, not unlike a chemistry test tube. This allowed for air to be funnelled from below the flame and created a better light and more efficient use of oil.

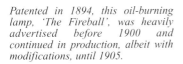

Patented in 1894, this oil-burning lamp, 'The Fireball', was heavily advertised before 1900 and continued in production, albeit with modifications, until 1905.

bicycle, it was not until the Defence of the Realm Act (DORA) was passed in 1915 that an illuminated red rear lamp became compulsory. After the First World War the act was repealed and, although the motoring lobby fought hard for its reinstatement, the Cyclists' Touring Club vigorously opposed any regulation that made the cyclist responsible for making himself visible to cars approaching from the rear at night. In April 1928 a statute was passed requiring rear lamps to be used on all vehicles during the hours of darkness.

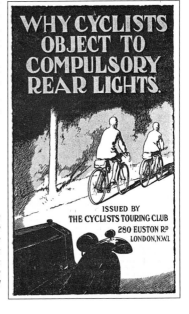

It is difficult to understand today, but in the early years of the twentieth century bicycle and tricycle riders, championed by the Cyclists' Touring Club, believed that it was the responsibility of motor-car drivers to see and avoid cyclists on the road. This booklet, issued in the early 1920s, offered a good case for the non-introduction of rear lamps; the effort was wasted, however, because by 1928 rear lamps on all vehicles had become statutory.

Powell & Hanmer often took the rear page of the Temple Press 'Cycling' magazine. The firm's advertisements – designed by Evan Jones – were often artistic and inspired, as in this case of a cycling platoon sergeant reading his orders by the light of a bicycle lamp during the First World War.

Acetylene gas lamps

During the last years of the nineteenth century some very inventive ideas were patented on both sides of the Atlantic featuring what was then called 'artificial daylight'. In 1892 two chemists, Willson and Moorehead, discovered the electric-furnace method of cheaply producing calcium carbide and demonstrated that the dripping of water on calcium carbide produced acetylene gas, which gave a brilliant white light when ignited. This new and exciting lighting medium encouraged frenetic development of vehicle lamps as well as of domestic and railway lighting. With the continued upsurge in cycling and cycling novelties, many small manufacturing companies believed that they had identified a business opportunity and some fascinating and bizarre designs were marketed.

A Brown & Smith 'White Star' acetylene gas lamp of 1899. The calcium carbide is stored in the lower container, held by a securing wire; the water reservoir is above; and the illumination head can be raised and lowered on the ridged burner support to allow for focusing.

Thomas Willson (1860–1915) devised the process for the commercial production of calcium carbide in 1892. A prolific inventor, he failed to maximise his patent rights in later years and the money he earned from carbide was mortgaged to finance new projects that failed to pay. He died penniless in New York.

An editorial in the American cycling magazine *The Hub* claimed that the first acetylene gas bicycle lamp was manufactured in 1895 by F. H. Fuller under the auspices of the Illinois Acetylene Company. The lamp appears to have been patented but it is not known if examples were actually produced. What is undoubted is that the Solar Acetylene Lamp Company (later renamed the Badger Brass Company) of Chicago advertised the first successful acetylene gas bicycle lamp in 1897 and named it the 'Solar'. It was manufactured until 1926 and was so popular that it has been estimated that some two million lamps were produced. Various attempts were made to copy the success of the 'Solar'. The Schumacher Acetylite Lamp Company brought out the 'Schumacher' and the Philadelphia Cycle Material Company the 'Helios', the latter claiming that its model would give a brilliant white light for ten hours. In England, J. G. A. Kitchen patented his

Left: *Introduced by the Union Lamp Company of Chicago in 1897, this kerosene-burning 'Boulevard' lamp, later named the 'Globe', possesses fifteen red, green, blue and opaque faceted glass 'jewels'. When lit, the effect is colourful and startling.*

Right: *Illustrated in a Desponts & Godfrey catalogue of 1900, this dual-purpose acetylene gas lamp was designed as a bicycle lamp that could also be used as a domestic table lamp if desired.*

Three versions of the 1898 Badger Brass Company 'Solar' together with a wooden delivery box and a 'Solar' sponsored calcium carbide tin. The 'Solar' lamp was the most successful of all the North American bicycle acetylene lamps. It was manufactured between 1897 and 1926, and its style was blatantly copied by many American and European companies, including Helios, Lucas, Riemann and Willocq-Bottin. The son of the company treasurer was Orson Welles, whose later fame was founded on his quality education paid for by the profits of the company.

'Manchester' lamp in April 1897 and L. S. Buffington patented his 'Buffington' lamp in October of the same year. The first commercially viable English lamp was the 'Acetylator'. Patented by Joseph Lucas Limited of Birmingham, this lamp was manufactured until 1902. By 1905 there was a large variety of acetylene gas lamps available to complement the many oil and kerosene examples.

Although their ability to produce a very powerful white light was impressive, acetylene gas-powered bicycle lamps never achieved acceptance with lady cyclists. One reason for this was the disagreeable odour emitted; another was the need to clean the sticky slaked lime or calcium hydroxide residue out of the carbide bowl after use. Add to this the awkward task of keeping the horsehair filter and burner free of dust, and it is not surprising that this form of lighting was popular

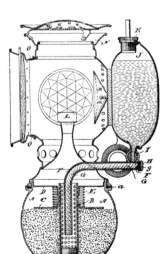

The 'Solar' was the first commercially available acetylene gas bicycle lamp, introduced by the Solar Acetylene Lamp Company in the United States in 1897. This cut-away profile of the 1899 version of the lamp shows the water in the upper chamber and calcium carbide in the lower container, with a cotton cord connecting the two reservoirs. The dry cord would allow water to filter down to the calcium carbide and acetylene gas would be produced. When the gas pressure increased, the water would not drain from the cord, the cord would therefore swell and the gas would be burned off at the burner, which lowered the pressure, in turn allowing the water to continue dripping. It was the appeal of this simple but effective automatic system of water control that helped popularise the 'Solar' lamp.

Perhaps now considered to be in dubious taste, in 1911, the date of this French advertising postcard, political correctness was not a consideration. Farcical themes were often used to underline the attributes of manufactured products, in this case the lighting power of the American 'Solar' acetylene gas lamp, strong enough to see a poacher stealing a chicken.

Right: A White Manufacturing Company 'Dupee' acetylene gas lamp of 1898. Before 1900 many ideas were patented in an effort to get the right amount of water to the calcium carbide without flooding the chamber. This lamp has inner and outer cylindrical chambers. Calcium carbide is put into the centre chamber and water in the outer chamber; a small hole connecting the two is supposed to allow water to pass. However, after a little while the sticky slaked lime residue tended to block the hole and inhibit water flow.

only with the most dedicated club rider. Nevertheless, an amazing number of styles and varieties were manufactured. While the most interesting examples fall into the period 1896–1915, acetylene gas-powered bicycle lamps were still being advertised until 1940.

After the First World War French manufacturers created acetylene bicycle lamps of robust yet simple design, as in the case of this 'Cicca' lamp dating from the 1930s. Similar acetylene gas lamps are still being manufactured in India.

A typical Art Deco hanging French advertisement for the 'Magondeaux' dissolved-acetylene bicycle lighting system. As the name suggests, the set comprises two units; the front projector and the dissolved-acetylene cylinder attached to the down-tube of the bicycle. The lady wearing a cloche hat gives the impression of middle-class acceptance of the medium, not to mention the cleanliness of its use.

Below: *A collection of transfer-printed tins for calcium carbide and burning oil dating from the early twentieth century.*

Candle lamps

Candle-powered lighting was never hugely popular with the cycling public and appears to have been a particularly European obsession, with very few references to candle-powered bicycle lamps in the United States. History demonstrates that this fuel medium made four distinct appearances before 1940.

It seems to have appeared first at the time of the Vélocipède craze. Lithographic images depict rather fanciful candle lamps fitted to the fronts of bicycles in about 1868. French and English Vélocipède manufacturers often included 'a lantern' as part of the list of requisites available to purchasers of machines. Some of the earliest references to their use appeared in publications such as the Andrew Muir of Salford catalogue of 1869, advertisements in the Peyton & Peyton 'Lamps and plated fittings' brochure of 1870 and an illustration of a lit lamp on a Vélocipède at night in *La Vélocipède Illustré* of January 1870. Without doubt they were crudely manufactured, especially when compared with later examples. They were provided simply as a lamp to be seen with rather than a lamp to see by.

Because of its cleanliness the candle lamp enjoyed a second revival in about 1892, when it provided an alternative fuel medium to the large oil-powered, tinplate lamps then available. By the mid 1890s these had ceased to be offered.

The candle lamp had its third wave of popularity from around 1900 until the start of the First World War. Powell & Hanmer and Henry Miller produced a number of examples, all artistically finished and undoubtedly designed to appeal to female cyclists.

An H. Miller & Company 'Talolite' candle-powered lamp dating from around 1905.

The fourth and last revival of interest in candle-powered lighting was during the 1930s, when cheaper examples were again offered as a compromise in times of austerity, particularly in France, Denmark and Holland.

Despite the advertising claims of power and reliability, the bicycle candle lamp emitted very little light and was almost impossible to keep burning, even in the lightest of breezes. Notwithstanding this, a number of attractive models were manufactured. Joseph Lucas made one model between 1901 and 1912, albeit with several design modifications; Powell & Hanmer produced two, the 'Oracle' and the 'Aerolite', from 1902 to 1914. European cyclists seem to have made more use of this lighting medium, with H. O. Asp of Copenhagen producing his uniquely shaped cylindrical lamps from 1900 until well into the 1930s, while Hermann Riemann of Germany produced a large number of models, usually of tinplate construction. Although not always named, these lamps can be recognised by an impressed oak-leaf trademark.

A Joseph Lucas Limited advertising poster dating from 1904 – an example of the cornucopia of 'Cyclealities' offered by the company during this period.

Candle lamps designed for use with bicycles survive in large numbers and many collectors assume – because of the simplicity of their design – that they all date from before 1914 or were used exclusively in Victorian times. On the contrary, many examples date from the 1930s revival period when French manufacturers exported inexpensive models, with trade names such as 'Cicca', 'Reiduar' and 'Luxor', for use not only on bicycles but also on small horse-drawn carts and hand barrows; indeed, they were advertised for use with perambulators until the 1950s.

Special candles were marketed for use in cycle candle lamps. They had to burn slowly without losing their firmness but at the same time be liquid enough to allow the upward pressure of the supporting spring to keep them in position. Some of the exotic substances used to create these candles have included oleo-stearine, carnauba wax, hardened whale oil and hardened bean oil.

Although designed to be ephemeral, colourful boxes looked attractive at the point of sale and manufacturers vied with each other to offer the most picturesque image, balanced against the cost of producing it.

Electric lamps

With the 1879 invention of the incandescent bulb by Thomas Edison in the United States and development work by Joseph Swan in England, by the time the first battery-operated bicycle lamp was introduced the principles of electricity, its benefits and its problems were all well recognised. Joseph Lucas & Sons manufactured a rechargeable battery-powered lamp in 1888 and, because of development costs, manufacture and royalty payments, marketed it for 55 shillings, a considerable price at the time. The lamp was advertised for little more than a year and few could have been sold. The battery lamp reappeared in 1893 with the 'Arabian' and again in 1896 with the 'Ohio', manufactured by the Cleveland company in the United States.

Dynamo-powered electric lighting was first introduced in about 1895 and descriptive names such as 'Dynolite' and 'Voltalite' appeared before 1900. The popularity of acetylene gas-powered lamps continued to eclipse the development of the electric lamp, not least because of the expense of manufacturing the electric bulb and its need for regular replacement because of its fragility. However, once the club riders realised that claims by the acetylene gas lamp makers of power and reliability were exaggerated, a slow increase in the demand for electric lighting continued until, by the start of the First World War, a number of models were being offered.

The company Ever Ready was a pioneer in the field. Originally incorporated in 1901 as the American Electrical Novelty and Manufacturing Company of London, the firm imported American goods that required dry cell batteries with the brand name 'Ever Ready'. With its trade booming, the company was re-floated as the British Ever Ready Electrical Company in 1906 and, although the company name has changed several times, the 'Ever Ready' brand is still associated with battery-powered cycle lighting.

A 1930s transfer-printed tin advertising shop sign, colourfully promoting the 'Star Melior' dynamo system.

A Pifco advertisement for both a bicycle horn and a self-contained battery-powered lamp.

In 1914 an artificial halt to the development of electric lighting was effected as a direct result of European governments not supporting electric lighting for military vehicles, favouring instead the trusty and well-established oil and acetylene lamps for use on military bicycles. After the war the manufacturing companies were wealthy enough to spend money on research and development. The efficiency of dynamos increased, batteries increased in power in proportion to their decrease in size and, more importantly, bulbs became mass-produced and inexpensive to buy. By the 1930s oil and acetylene lamps, although still being manufactured, had been largely superseded by the many lightweight electric battery and dynamo lamps on offer.

Lamp names

One of the charms of collecting early cycle lamps is that they were frequently labelled with interesting names. Indeed, manufacturers strove to popularise their products by giving each model a unique name. Some of the names were meaningful, such as 'The Long Distance Lamp', 'Reliance' and 'The Tourist'; others were patriotic, for example 'The Rob Roy', 'Cock O' the Walk' and 'Arlington'; and others were imaginative, including 'Unique', 'Cetolite' and 'Acetylator'. Equally importantly, the names had a dual commercial

Lohmann's 'Perfecta Nova' acetylene gas lamp. Dating from 1901, this lamp is one of a whole series of 'Perfecta' lamps from the German company. The acetylene gas generated was delivered to the burner by the visible rubber tubing; this also helped cool the gas before it was burned at the burner tip.

Right: *An 1897 Bridgeport Brass Company 'Searchlight' oil-lamp advertisement in the form of a baseball ticket, in this case unused with the coupon still attached. This highly attractive embossed lamp was offered until just before 1914.*

purpose. Firstly, when a rider was out on a club ride, recommendation and praise of a lamp were more memorable when given by name rather than by number. Secondly, as most local hardware stores could not afford to carry a large stock of lamps, it was convenient for lamps to be ordered direct from the manufacturer by their names. How much more eloquent, too, the customer felt when able to walk into a local shop and ask for a 'New Sunray please' rather than simply say, 'I am looking for a pleasing lamp'!

Automobile lighting

Karl Benz invented the first practical self-propelled motor vehicle in 1885 and as early as 1888 Wilhelm Maybach was driving a Daimler with candle-powered coach lamps attached. Victorian motorists seldom ventured out after dark because their vehicles were so unreliable. Before 1900 lamps were fitted to cars more for decorative reasons than functional ones. However, as reports of European motor-car trials, particularly those that included a certain amount of night driving, made an impression on the motoring public, so longer and longer journeys were undertaken and driving after dark became a curiosity. Many motorists fitted bicycle lamps to their cars and the cycle-lamp manufacturers obliged by creating lamps with slightly larger wicks and reflectors in an attempt to produce a better light. However, their weak and inadequate mounting brackets often disintegrated because they were unable to cope with the vibration caused by faster speeds and treacherous road surfaces.

Just as production car rallies and trials highlight weaknesses in new models today, so the European racing events affected the development of useful vehicle lighting. In 1894 the French magazine *Le Petit Journal* started to sponsor competitions. During the first

A Louis Blériot advertising postcard showing two men comparing the attributes of their new lamp.

— Toi si morose... tu as l'air **rayonnant**
— Ce qui prouve mon cher la puissance d'éclairage de l'**Éclaireur BLÉRIOT**

An advertisement for a late-nineteenth-century self-contained acetylene head-lamp. The price of 120 shillings (£6) represented almost a year's wages for some workers.

'OTTO" HEAD LIGHT.

NO. 21.

This Lamp has been constructed to answer similar requirements to those best known to the trade, but in the "OTTO" are embodied many special features and improvements, not the least of which is the possibility of detaching and interchanging all parts. It is a handsome and strongly made lamp, giving perfect results.

Price **120/-**

Weight complete 13-lbs.   Diam. of Lens 6½-ins.

Burns about six hours

event almost all of the entrants had difficulty in keeping their frail oil and candle lamps intact, let alone alight. By the time of the Paris to Ostend race of 1899, only purpose-made oil and acetylene gas lamps were in use.

As vehicles became faster, a need for more powerful lamps arose. A new lighting medium then finding favour in large country houses was acetylene gas and in consequence much progress on that front had already been achieved. Of the many pioneers in the development of motor-vehicle lamps, Henry Salsbury and his father Edward were among the most successful, with their business in the heart of the coach-building trade in Long Acre, London. Louis Blériot of Paris had also been experimenting with acetylene gas lamps since 1896

The shop-front of the Louis Blériot factory and shop at 14–16 Rue Duret in Paris around 1908.

The power claims for early vehicle lighting were sometimes quite outrageous. This Jean Roose advertisement of 1903 implies that a whole town, maybe his home town of Brussels, could be illuminated from a single vantage-point by one of his acetylene gas-powered headlamps.

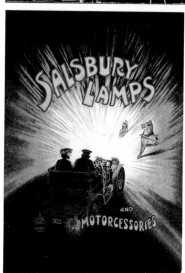

Left: *Henry Salsbury encouraged spirited and exciting advertising for his products, no more so than in this 1905 advertisement depicting the motor car as a potent force, with its lamps outshining the horse in public esteem.*

and in 1899 he collaborated with Henry Salsbury in the manufacture of what was to be the first successful automobile lamp. Named the 'Salsbury-Blériot', these lamps were assembled in London from high-quality spun-brass parts and distributed through the Blériot depots located around mainland Europe and the Salsbury franchises in England.

These headlamps worked on the self-contained principle; that is, they produced acetylene gas from a mixture of calcium carbide and water within the body of the lamp itself. Being a self-contained unit, the lamp differed from the later development of an acetylene gas generator feeding, through a rubber tube and copper piping, a separately mounted projector headlamp.

Joseph Lucas Limited, whose factory was in Birmingham, was one of the first manufacturers to incorporate solid brackets and vibration-

The rear yard and entrance archway of the Joseph Lucas factory in Little King Street, Birmingham, where, in the last years of the nineteenth century, some of the first motor-car side lamps and headlamps were designed and tested. Harry Lucas's office was on the ground floor; there he kept his drawing board and could also keep an eye on the comings and goings of the workers and the goods they produced.

proof components in its motor lamps. Its first oil lamp specifically designed for the use of 'Autorists' was called a 'motor carriage lamp'. Priced at 50 shillings (£2.50) a pair, these lamps were the first of their type to be symmetrically sided. This meant that as well as having a 5 inch (125 mm) diameter double convex lens to the front, each lamp incorporated a square bevelled-edge glass on the outer flank so that a radiance of light would give a warning to traffic approaching from the side. At the end of 1904 rear lamps shining a red light from the back of the vehicle to warn oncoming traffic began to be encouraged by the local courts, although not in every county of England.

Early oil-burning lamps did not project a very effective light to the road. Indeed, their only requirement was to indicate a vehicle's presence to other road users. Street lighting, particularly in the larger towns, became more widespread so drivers tended to use their oil lamps for town work only. For country work, larger and more imposing lamps were added – particularly on cars that were maintained by a chauffeur, since it was a laborious task to keep the

Right: *A J. R. Oldfield manufactured oil-powered rear lamp. These lamps were produced from about 1904, when some English counties insisted on rear illumination at night. However, this requirement was by no means universal and it did not become obligatory throughout Europe and the United States until the 1920s.*

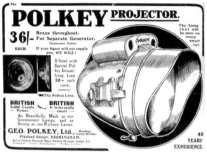

Above: *George Polkey was a manufacturer of inspired imagination and high standards. Like so many lamp manufacturers, his roots were based in domestic lighting but he conveniently turned to motor-vehicle lighting when oil-powered lighting for the home went into decline at the end of the nineteenth century.*

lamps clean, topped up with fuel and ready for use. The market-place was steadily growing and it is estimated that by 1905 there were more than forty large companies throughout the world, as well as many hundreds of smaller companies, offering an amazing diversity of lamps and fittings.

The American manufacturer Samuel Rushmore made a significant contribution to the increase of candlepower for vehicle lamps. He realised that to achieve a good beam the reflected rays of light needed

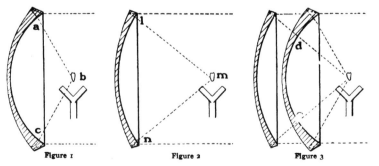

One of the first lamp manufacturers to incorporate a scientifically designed rear reflector was Samuel Rushmore in the United States. As this diagram shows, exact parallelism of rays is achieved by refracting the beam through a silver-backed glass reflector of increasing thickness towards the edges. By using this device, the burner can be adjusted horizontally in order to change the width and density of the beam on the road.

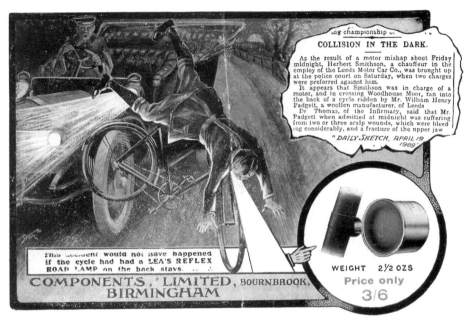

Collisions between motorists and cyclists at night had long been a problem but cyclists tended to resist the motorists' call for them to display a rear lamp, mainly because of its expense. In 1908 R. H. Lea patented a cheap rear reflector that he named the 'Reflex Road Light', which did find favour with cyclists and probably saved many lives.

to be as parallel as possible and adapted a special type of reflector. Originally devised by a French engineer, Colonel Mangin, it used a heat-resistant silver-backed glass reflector of increasing thickness towards the edges. This allowed for an exact parallelism of rays by refracting the light beam to the road, the strength of the beam being considerably better than that of its American competitors. Unfortunately, the reflectors were expensive to produce and were fitted into rather plain cylindrical-style lamps that found little favour with European drivers. The company had disappeared by 1918.

Joseph Lucas used the trade name 'King of the Road' on bicycle lamps from 1879. The name soon came to epitomise top-of-the-range manufacture, so the firm used it on many of its better-quality motor lamps as well, the first to bear the epithet being introduced in 1902. This was a self-contained lamp, using a similar paraffin-coated calcium carbide to that used by the earlier 'Salsbury-Blériot' lamp. It was, on the other hand, heavy and difficult to control. A carrying bail was incorporated so that the lamp could be lifted away from the car while the coachwork was being washed.

In the chairman's report at the 1904 annual general meeting of Joseph Lucas Limited, Harry Lucas announced to enraged shareholders that the dividends for that financial year were limited because of development costs of the 'new motor lighting requisites'.

SECTIONAL DRAWING

OF THE

"King of the Road" Headlight.

A Gas.
B Water.
C Coated Carbide.
D Gas Bag.
E Gas to Burner.

F Gas-tight Seating.
G Condensing & Cooling Chamber.
H Draining Screw.
J Plug Tap.
K Gas purifier.

Joseph Lucas Limited was aware that its market-place was dominated by landed gentry, who, it was believed, would find it difficult to comprehend the principles of acetylene gas. In its 1904 catalogue the firm published a sectionalised diagram of its first 'King of the Road' headlamp in an attempt to dispel the mystique and popularise this lighting medium.

Below: *A matched pair of Badger Brass Company 'Solar' acetylene gas lamps dating from 1905. Note the calcium carbide housing cylinders below the water reservoir, the carrying bail and the centrally positioned condenser lens to aid light intensity.*

An unusual 1914 advertisement for the firm Auteroche of Paris, which has employed the hands of 'Responsibility' and 'Security' to persuade drivers to take their task seriously and purchase only the best lighting available.

The money was well spent, since in 1905 the most profitable variation of the 'King of the Road' appeared. It incorporated a new and refreshingly simple water-regulation device, or drip-feed, which allowed the driver to achieve improved control over gas production, and consequently over the strength of beam emitted. Its popularity was also helped by the fact that the Lucas design was less wasteful and that inexpensive ordinary lump calcium carbide could be used.

By looking at the annual returns for the major lamp manufacturers in both Europe and the United States we can see that by 1907 there was a slump in trade. The surge of enthusiasm for the motor car was starting to diminish; those car owners with mounted lighting equipment were pleased with its efficiency and, more importantly, its longevity and some motorists would move their lamps from car to car, simply remounting them on a replacement vehicle as the need arose. In consequence some lamp-manufacturing companies disappeared, for example Worsnop's of Halifax and Alfred Russell of Walsall. Salsbury of London was forced into bankruptcy and re-floated with a new share capital in 1909.

Electric lamps

All the principles of successful electrical lighting were available by 1890; indeed, the streets of New York were ablaze with incandescent lights. On the face of it the same illumination principles could have

Despite the increased availability of electrically powered lighting, owners of oil lamps were reluctant to change their lamps, so several manufacturers produced an electric bulb adapter for use in oil-powered side lamps.

Below: *Colour advertising was rare before the First World War but trained commercial artists were adept at producing excellent monochrome advertisements, as in the case of this example promoting CAV electric motor-car lighting.*

been applied to motor vehicles, but the major problem was the delicacy of the glass bulb, particularly the carbon filament.

Charles Anthony Vandervell began manufacturing electrical fittings in 1892. By 1900, after gaining considerable experience with railway lighting, he had begun to advocate the use of electrical lighting for the motor car and went into production of electric side lamps in 1901; the Daimler Company adopted these lamps as standard fittings a year later. The motoring press and the public started to compare the properties of the glass bulb with those of powerful acetylene gas and found the low-wattage electric bulbs to be weak and, given the vibrations of the road, to have a short working life. By 1903, although Vandervell's products were often fitted to electrically powered town cars, thereby utilising the available energy source, high-wattage headlamps were not viable because of the amount of energy needed to supply a continuous strong beam. From about 1904 an auxiliary power source, a dynamo, was often attached to the engine, but because a vehicle's speed and, consequently, the engine speed varied, an accumulator, later called a battery, was utilised as a buffer to help stabilise the fluctuations in current.

Wiring had also to keep pace with developments. Before 1903 single wires sheathed in cotton, helically coiled to combat vibration, were stretched between brass terminals.

After this time wires, all separate but positioned side by side, were clipped together in straight lines to the underside of the body and chassis frame. With more expensive cars that required a wire to pass through a component or chassis member, metal-armoured wires with spring-loaded contacts at the ends allowed them to be screwed into the relevant tube. As the complexity of the lamps, dynamo and components grew, bundling together a large number of wires, the potential for fraying and damage increased; this could be alleviated by creating a wiring loom that encased the wires in a woven cotton fabric.

Another drawback to electric lighting was its expense. A medium-sized installation would cost about £35. This would include not only the purchase of the lamps but also the employment of a capable engineer to fit a pulley system to the engine to drive the dynamo. An accumulator had to be securely fitted, the head and side lamps needed stout brackets, and all had to be carefully wired to a multiple switch box attached to the dashboard. Only the wealthiest vehicle owners could afford such a system and as a result the relative simplicity of oil and acetylene continued to be the favoured sources of lighting.

The motor-car lamp assembly shop at the C. A. Vandervell & Company Electrical Engineers' factory in Acton Vale, London, in 1911.

An Imperial German limousine, possibly an NAG, with Zeiss acetylene gas lamps fitted and, for embellishment, miniature depictions of the state crown fitted on each of the heat cowls.

By 1910 firms such as Gray & Davis and Westinghouse in the United States and Carl Zeiss and Rotax in Europe were all producing economic electrical lighting systems. At about this time the delicate carbon filament in the glass bulb was changed to a more robust tungsten filament. The glass bulb was now not only capable of withstanding the energetic vibrations created by the road surface but, more importantly, the standard 4 volt bulb could endure an increase in dynamo power and, consequently, an increase in wattage and candlepower.

An alternative to acetylene generated by carbide was compressed bottled acetylene. This achieved limited success on large touring cars and commercial vehicles.

The medium was gaining commercial ground until the outbreak of hostilities in 1914, when the War Office turned its attention to motoring contracts. Surprisingly, and in contradiction to progressive thinking, the Ministry of Defence insisted on oil- and acetylene-powered lighting equipment being fitted to its vehicles. The firm of Powell & Hanmer, which had resisted change and had not tooled up for

Francis Hanmer (1858–1925), photographed in 1903. He was co-founder in 1884 of the Powell & Hanmer Lamp Company. Both Francis Hanmer and Frank Powell were keen cyclists and belonged to the Centaur Bicycle Club, through which no doubt they promoted their wares and tested new models. From 1905 Powell wanted to spend profits on the development of electric lighting for motor cars but Hanmer resisted and by 1910 Powell had consequently sold his interests in the company.

An interior view of S. Smith & Son's newly opened showroom in Great Portland Street, London, in about 1911. Note the various lamps and motoring accessories in cabinets around the walls and a mock-up of a Daimler motor car demonstrating the fitting and positioning of lamps, dynamo and accessories.

During the First World War the War Office encouraged the use of oil and acetylene lighting on its military vehicles. This 3 ton Napier truck has a pair of J. R. Oldfield oil-powered side lamps fitted and, on the nearside, a Powell & Hanmer acetylene gas lamp, the latter with a rudimentary light-inhibiting white disc to reduce the likelihood of being spotted by enemy aircraft at night.

A pair of Stephen Grebel electric projectors. During their fifteen-year period of manufacture from 1923 these French lamps retained the same basic spherical style, with matching projectors, spot lamps and side lamps, and found particular favour with the French Art Deco coachbuilders.

A pair of Marchal electric projectors dating from around 1932. Note the stout brackets either side for mounting to fast sports cars and the dipped-beam subsidiary plano-lens and small electric bulb cup behind.

electricity, now found itself in favour and was one of the chief suppliers to the War Department, stealing a march on its forward-thinking contemporaries. The company produced a range of uninspired and bland designs of vehicle and auxiliary lighting that can usually be found today with 'WD' embossed on their heat cowls.

By the 1920s vehicle speeds had increased and night driving was commonplace. Returning war heroes demanded luxuries, fuelling inflation. Experiments were carried out to develop inexpensive lighting equipment that was simple to use, and this was soon routinely fitted on most leading models. Manufacturers were able to purchase in bulk and started to include lamps on their cars as a design feature to complement the styling rather than merely as a useful accessory.

Stephen Grebel in Paris was one of the first manufacturers to promote electric lamp design. From 1924 all of his lamp styles incorporated the same distinctive spherical shape. They were built of high-quality spun brass with stout pillar or fork mounting brackets and were superbly finished in nickel-plating, changing to chromium-plating after 1928. He offered headlamps, wing lamps and hand-controlled spot lamps, each with the manufacturer's name etched into the front convex glass.

The illuminating power of electric lamps had greatly increased during the 1920s. Not only had the wattage of the bulbs increased, but reflectors also became more scientifically correct. Time and money were spent on research, the primary change being to the parabolic reflector, which was brought right around the bulb and shaped to form the rear reflector in a single combination unit. As more and more motor vehicles took to the road headlight dazzle continued to be a major problem. Various attempts were made to reduce the glare caused by the headlamps of approaching cars because this often caused drivers and pedestrians to be temporarily blinded, resulting in frequent accidents.

Dazzle

Until the early 1930s, when significant road improvements were undertaken, the countryside was very dark at night, with little street

As early as 1910 lamp manufacturer Carl Zeiss tackled the mechanical elimination of glare caused by acetylene gas lamps. A dipping mechanism was placed near the driver and connected by Bowden cable to a perforated cup hinged to the front of the burner. When raised, this effectively reduced the intensity of the burner.

lighting even on the busiest of roads. As early as 1905 acetylene gas-powered lamps, having gained in popularity, highlighted the problem of dazzle and many minds were occupied in attempting to resolve the issue.

Early ideas were legion – some inspired, some practical and some ridiculous. They often focused on the light source – the acetylene gas burner itself – and varied from the activation of vented cups enclosing the burner to manually operated shutters behind the front glass. Other ideas included anti-glare screens hung over the windscreen, anti-glare spectacles for the driver and moulded anti-dazzle glass lenses.

During 1921 the first institutionally approved step towards curing glare was devised by W. Fenson in the United States. He invented a mechanism by which the front lamps were mounted on hinges and could be dropped forward by means of a cable attached to the dashboard. In England a dipping-headlight system was patented by Barker and marketed from 1923 as 'Barker Dippers'. An extra lever, not dissimilar to a gear lever, was placed by the driver's right hand. When pushed forward in response to an oncoming car, a long bar was activated that dipped both headlamps to the road surface with a comforting thud, thus shielding the oncoming driver from a blinding glare. When the road ahead was clear the lever was pulled back and the headlamps returned to their normal position. One drawback was that the stiffness of the lever, with the full weight of the lamps attached, promoted driver fatigue. Nevertheless, the system was highly successful and motor-car manufacturers as varied as Morris and Rolls-Royce offered it as an optional extra.

Another difficulty with visibility was that if a series of oncoming cars was approaching the edge of the road ahead would be plunged into complete darkness, making it doubly difficult for the driver to see where he was going. In 1928 a semi-rotary dipper was designed with

During the 1930s electric bulbs and road signs were an everyday part of the motoring scene.

the effect that the headlamps dipped and twisted to the nearside kerb of the road, making driving against oncoming traffic much safer.

The first simple anti-glare device was the 'dipping reflector', which was patented and introduced by Joseph Lucas Limited in 1927. This took the form of a pneumatic cylinder and control knob mounted on the steering column, and was connected by rubber tubing to a small pneumatic cylinder in each headlamp. When the knob was pulled out a piston in each lamp moved the reflector into a diagonally dipped position, throwing the beam of light on to the nearside kerb. This enabled drivers to see both pedestrians and oncoming cars. In 1930 there was a further improvement that helped to reduce the combined strength of the beam; this was descriptively referred to as 'dip and switch'. The reflectors were now attached to a solenoid. Activated by a switch on the dashboard or steering column, the nearside lamp dipped to the kerb in the usual way but the offside headlamp was switched off, leaving the side lamps to reveal the width of the vehicle. Although this device was popular in Britain, the European manufacturers such as Bosch, Marchal and Zeiss favoured the newly developed double-filament bulb.

Major A. Graves patented a double-filament or 'dipping' electric bulb as early as 1924. One of the filaments was placed at the best focal point of the optical system to provide a long straight beam. The other filament was placed ahead of or above the first filament to allow for an out-of-focus spread of light to the road. The filaments had separate contacts in the brass collar of the bulb and could be switched alternately by either a foot-operated or a hand-operated switch. The Lucas-Graves double-filament bulb appeared around 1928. This was expensive and, as it turned out, not widely popular in Britain. Only Austin and Vauxhall Motors seem to have used it as standard equipment, although it was fitted by other manufacturers for export cars only. Alternatives were available in the shape of the single-filament bulbs of Osram and MEP. These were pigment-coated on the top half of the bulb, with the result that all upward rays of light were diffused, preventing dazzle from a considerable distance.

An advertising postcard for Paul Gadot of Paris from just before the First World War offering electrical bulbs and auxiliary lamps to the motorist.

Being blinded by the dazzling lights of oncoming cars became a major problem for motorists as lamps became more powerful. In 1908 Salsbury designed the appropriately named 'Anti-Dazlo' glass lenses and for a while eased the eye strain of all road users, as promoted in this advertising postcard dated 1910.

Royal Automobile Club lamp trials

Reports from Faraday House, the original headquarters of the Institution of Electrical Engineers, on the effectiveness and use of motor-vehicle lighting had appeared by 1908, but perhaps the most detailed were those of the Royal Automobile Club. In 1909, under royal patronage, the club organised a series of tests on both anti-dazzle devices and illumination effectiveness. The standard adopted by the judges for an effective range of light was 20 candlepower and, in the case of acetylene gas, consumption was not to exceed 7 cubic feet (2.1 cubic metres) of gas per hour using 2.8 ounces (79 grams) of calcium carbide. Other parameters were involved but the winner, much to the chagrin of Joseph Lucas Limited, which viewed itself as the leader in the field, was Henry Salsbury of London. In 1921 the Royal Automobile Club organised another series of tests and Salsbury again gave a good performance, although, ironically, the firm had ceased meaningful manufacture of vehicle lighting before the First World War and was in receivership by 1921.

The five-lamp set

From the early days of motoring it had been a matter of personal preference exactly where lamps were fitted on a vehicle. While oil and electric lamps were normally fitted to the sides of the car and either one or two headlamps fitted to the front, this was not obligatory.

Politicians and local government had always been concerned about the alarming number of road accidents and tried many times to enact laws that regulated vehicle lighting and lamps, particularly rear lamps. With the ever-increasing numbers of motor vehicles road fatalities increased annually until, in 1929, the 'five-lamp set' became statutory. This regulation established the use and positioning of two parking or side lamps, two evenly positioned headlamps and a combined rear number-plate light, rear lamp and stop lamp to be fitted to the offside rear of the car. This lighting standard for all three- and four-wheeled vehicles remained in place until 1939.

Sealed beams

The Thompson-Houston Company, in 1937, was the first to develop the sealed-beam unit after realising that the accurate focusing of the filaments and the maintenance of a clean reflector were best accomplished in a tamper-proof environment. The General Electric Company (GEC) in the United States developed the concept further, creating, in effect, a large bulb in which the filament was sealed into the back of a glass reflector and the front glass was sealed to the reflector rim, the whole being filled with an inert gas.

The 1930s was the decade of motoring for the masses. Reliability and convenience replaced uncertainty and discomfort and, as they have done throughout the long history of motoring, the performance and effectiveness of the mounted lighting equipment played a very important part. Modern motor-vehicle lighting has its roots in the early 1920s, when lamps were first included as part of the styling of a vehicle rather than as a necessary adjunct. By 1939 lamps which amounted to little more than glass-covered reflectors were flush-fitted into the bodywork of most vehicles, although some sports cars and coach-built cars such as Rolls-Royce, Bentley and MG carried on using separately mounted lamps until well after the Second World War.

Surprisingly, oil side lamps and acetylene-powered lamps continued to be manufactured until 1939, particularly for use on a wide variety of commercial vehicles, from handcarts to traction engines. Some European manufacturers such as Hella and Cicca still offered simple carriage candle lamps for use on farm vehicles until after the Second World War.

United Motor Industries was a predatory company set up by investors to encroach on the profitable motoring accessories market. Under the trading name of 'Castle', the firm had its goods manufactured by others and priced them to undercut the established brands. Its success was limited and little was heard of the company after 1914.

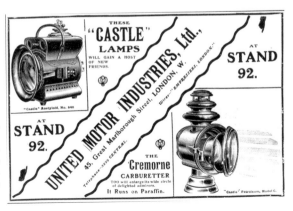

Finding and using old vehicle lamps

Since the 1960s, when the veteran and vintage vehicle scene developed into the multinational hobby it is today, old vehicle lamps have become sought after by collectors. Although examples from before the First World War are becoming harder to find, later lamps of all types are still easy to track down. The best hunting grounds are the many autojumbles that are held throughout Britain and abroad. If you are seeking lighting equipment for an American car, the best place to search is at the annual Hershey Swap Meet held in Pennsylvania every October. Should French products take your fancy, then the Retromobile in Paris every February will make for a fascinating visit. Some auction houses hold regular sales of automobilia and the lamp collector will find these as fruitful as antique fairs and shops.

Part of the pleasure of owning lamps, whether fitted to a vehicle or displayed in the home, is to be gained from using them. Acetylene gas and oil lamps offer the most fun; however, you may wish to heed a word of warning about oil lamps. Collectors often use modern paraffin

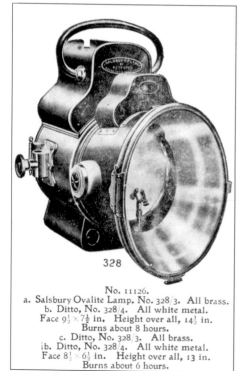

328

No. 11126.
a. Salsbury Ovalite Lamp. No. 328/3. All brass.
b. Ditto, No. 328/4. All white metal.
Face 9½ × 7¼ in. Height over all, 14½ in.
Burns about 8 hours.
c. Ditto, No. 328/3. All brass.
ib. Ditto, No. 328/4. All white metal.
Face 8½ × 6½ in. Height over all, 13 in.
Burns about 6 hours.

The Salsbury 'Ovalite' self-contained acetylene gas headlamp was highly successful before 1905 but soon disappeared from the motoring scene as lighting became more sophisticated and less imposing.

in their old oil lamps, which is entirely the wrong thing to do. Paraffin will quickly tarnish the reflector and leave a thick sooty deposit in the upper heat cowl. This happens because paraffin produced before the Second World War was a refined burning oil, while modern paraffin is a heating medium and is not designed to be an illuminating source. By far the best fuel available today is domestic lamp oil purchased from one of the many household warehouses. Make sure that a clean open-weave wick is used and that it is cut slightly curved to allow for a well-shaped flame.

Acetylene is a hydrocarbon gas produced by the action of dripping water on calcium carbide. Gas, being lighter than air, will rise via a burner to be lit with a match, giving a bright, almost blinding, white light. In the past calcium carbide was available in two types, coated and uncoated. Now only one universal type is obtainable and can be found in outdoor-pursuits shops, which sell it for use in potholing lamps. Although coated in paraffin to slow down the reaction process, it is similar to the uncoated variety in that it is supplied in small, easy-to-use pieces. If calcium carbide is stored in a dry atmosphere and in an airtight tin, then it will stay in good condition, but if it is kept in a damp place then an exothermic reaction will take place, causing it to degenerate.

An amusing electric rear light depicting a street 'dandy' with a bulb holder and a red-faceted glass in his body. These were fitted to the rear of Parisian wine-delivery lorries after the First World War.

Acetylene gas lamp burners

There are two types of acetylene gas lamp burner: atmospheric and non-atmospheric. In the latter a deposit of carbon will slowly form on the hot burner tip. This not only shortens the life of the burner but also necessitates frequent cleaning. Atmospheric burners, although more expensive, mix oxygen with the acetylene gas as it travels to the burner tip, which serves to cool the tip and helps to produce a clean, bright white light.

While the physical appearance of many burners appears to be similar, inspection of the metal collar will reveal that they variously carry the impressions '7-litre', '14-litre', '35-litre' and so on. This refers to the consumption rate per hour under maximum conditions.

As many acetylene gas burners are boat-shaped, the tendency to fit burners in headlamps parallel to the front glass is incorrect. The correct position is at a tangent to the front glass and rear reflector. In this way, as the two jets of flame meet at the centre they pan out to shine the maximum amount of reflected light on to the road ahead.

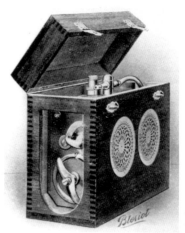

The claims of manufacturers of acetylene gas lighting were often exaggerated. 'Can be used repeatedly without being recharged' was a frequent claim, which today can be proved practically impossible.

Left: *With the introduction of acetylene gas lighting for motor cars in 1897, a subsidiary trade in fixtures such as burners became necessary. Atmospheric burners like those depicted used small vent holes in the sides of the burners to allow air to be mixed with the acetylene gas as it burned. Although these burners were more expensive than the non-atmospheric type, they were more efficient and lasted longer.*

Further information

Many transport museums have lamps on display. These are usually attached to vehicles rather than forming a cohesive display. Frequently the lamps mounted are inappropriate in both period and style and, more importantly, if captions are attached they tend to be factually inaccurate. There are a number of private collections around the world, mainly kept by enthusiasts who care about vehicle and lighting history. The Internet has a number of websites that include vehicle lighting and members of the Veteran Car Club and Veteran Cycle Club are usually very helpful in response to enquiries about lighting.

Useful addresses

Veteran Car Club of Great Britain, Jessamine Court, 15 High Street, Ashwell, Hertfordshire SG7 5NL. Telephone: 01462 742818. Website: www.vccofgb.co.uk

Veteran Cycle Club, Membership Secretary, 44 Springfield Road, Moseley, Birmingham B13 9NW. Website: www.v-cc.org.uk

Please visit the website: www.websolutionswa.com/pwc/ecl.asp which contains a good potted history of cycle lighting, photographs and discussion pages.

Places to visit

Beamish, The North of England Open Air Museum, Beamish, County Durham DH9 0RG. Telephone: 0191 370 4000. Website: www.beamish.org.uk

British Motor Industries Heritage Centre, Banbury Road, Gaydon, Warwickshire CV35 0BJ. Telephone: 01926 641188. Website: www.heritage.org.uk

Cotswold Motor Museum, The Old Mill, Bourton-on-the-Water, Gloucestershire GL54 2BY. Telephone: 01451 821255. Website: www.cotswold-motor-museum.com

Coventry Transport Museum, Millennium Place, Hales Street, Coventry CV1 1PN. Telephone: 024 7683 2465. Website: www.transport-museum.com

Dansk Cykel and Knallert Museum, DCM's Venner, Godthabsvej 247, 2720 Vanlose, Denmark.

Museum of Historic Cycling, The Old Station, Camelford, Cornwall PL39 9TZ. Telephone: 01840 212811.

Museum of Irish Transport, Scotts Hotel Gardens, Killarney, County Kerry, Ireland. Telephone: 00353 (0) 64 32638. Website: www.gleneaglehotel.com/transmues.htm

National Cycle Museum, The Automobile Palace, Temple Street, Llandrindod Wells, Powys LD1 5DL. Telephone: 01597 825531. Website: www.cyclemuseum.org.uk

National Fietsmuseum Velorama, Waalkade 107, 6511 XR Nijmegen, Netherlands. Telephone: 0031 (0) 2432 25851. Website: ww.velorama.nl

National Motor Museum, John Montagu Building, Beaulieu, Brockenhurst, Hampshire SO42 7ZN. Telephone: 01590 612345. Website: www.beaulieu.co.uk

National Museum of Scotland, Chambers Street, Edinburgh EH1 1JF. Telephone: 0131 247 4422. Website: www.nms.ac.uk

Pedaling History Bicycle Museum, 3943 North Buffalo Road, Orchard Park, New York NY14127-1841, USA. Telephone: 001 (0) 716 662 3853. Website: www.pedalinghistory.com

Lamps of an inappropriate period are often fitted to old motor cars today. This Powell & Hanmer self-contained acetylene gas lamp dates from 1910 but is wrongly mounted to a veteran car of 1903.

Index